No Running on the Boardwalk

NO RUNNING ON THE BOARDWALK

Paul Ramsey

The University of Georgia Press, Athens

Library of Congress Catalog Card Number: 74-75941
International Standard Book Number: 0-8203-0356-9
The University of Georgia Press, Athens 30602
Copyright © 1975 by Paul Ramsey
Printed in the United States of America

This book is for my mother
and in memory of my father

Contents

Acknowledgments

The author and the publisher gratefully acknowledge permission to reprint these poems which originally appeared in the publications here noted: "Images for the Gospel of Christ," *Approach;* "The Angels," *Award Winning Poems, 1967: Rochester Festival of Religious Arts;* "Ascension," *Descant;* "The Heart Dark-All-Round," *Epoch;* "A Convalescence," *Folio;* "Treasure," *four quarters;* "In a Cedar Wind," *International Who's Who in Poetry Anthology, 1973;* "The Edge of the City," *Malahat Review;* "Suppose a Country Gave a Holiday and Then Suppose That the Tears Were True," *Poetry;* "A Bank of Laurel," *Poetry Florida And;* "A Baker's Dozen for a Summer Town," *Quarterly Review of Literature;* "An Evening Colloquy," *St. Andrew's Cross;* "The Advance" and "The Progress," *Shenandoah;* "A Breastplate" and "Fog Days for Great Cranberry Island," *Southern Poetry Review;* "The Broken Lumber," *Tennessee Poetry Journal.* "Antiphon" has been set to music by Alec Wyton, former organist and master of choristers, the Cathedral Church of St. John the Divine, New York, and published as music by the Agápe Press.

A Baker's Dozen for a Summer Town

The town? What of the town? It is there still,
Violet waste of neon. What of that?
I have not seen you since. Time is to kill.
I hate the town. What are you getting at?

The time and place were summer in a town
Well known for summer loves, sun, sand, and sea.
New suns ascended on the running down
Of more than our intent. The clock was we.

The pilings' shadows hid us when we kissed,
Our raw souls nourishing their raw delight.
The boardwalk's tarry ooze in a thin mist
Is what I dream of, nightmare after night.

Quick music fed our love. Hangovers sank
Into our nervous systems like a storm.
It was the town's discourtesy we drank.
Was there no other way of keeping warm?

One day we saw a dead shark on the beach,
A small grey hammerhead. Men stood about
And whispered it. Its death was out of reach.
The white sharks swam in silence further out.

Sleep sank us down into a place of sleep
To breathe at ease a mild familiar air,
To scent the blankness of the wide and deep
And barren field of death. We sought us there.

1

A mile inland we walked to get away
From tyranny of water, from the pain
Of breakers edging on the clouded day.
Your lips were salt in a cold edge of rain.

The cards I held were bad. I played them worse.
I lost two hundred dollars. Then I quit.
You met me with a question. Edgy. Terse.
The quarreling was not to answer it.

The dunes were mirrors of the sun's expanse.
We dove in water till the sun was hid,
Then rose in spray and laughter, in pure dance.
What afternoon could offer night undid.

The resolution of the sea-light fell
Upon us like a nervous splash of foam.
The rains came after. Insolent as Hell,
The gate attendant asked where we came from.

You brushed your hair slowly and I watched you.
The mirror where your body curved to breast
Was the clear semblance of my wanting you.
You turned and you unsmilingly undressed.

The cigarettes and beer shifted, shifted.
We talked of other things. Too much was salt
In that dank air. About us were the dead
And they were drinking. Someone was at fault.

If I should tell, what word has not been let?
If I should spy whatever is to shun,
What then? What then? The memory is set.
No Running on the Boardwalk! Still we run.

The Advance

Against refusals you prepared a standard recitation.
In the haven of February you carried a bottle of silence,
Its smoke almost invisible in the prevalence of sunlight.
When you were asked for your name, you hesitated,
      and then you remembered and began to tremble and
      began to call on your forebears, whose boots
      resounded in the thicket among the castaway rusted
      steam valves and the revoked calling cards and if
      there was no succor why were you smiling or did you
      understand wrongly?
The rivers slide in the valleys away from the houses and echoes.

The Askers Ask the Day

Who are you, O Shining One?

I carry the sticks of winter in the rain.
I gather the seeds from hillsides long since sown.
I place a steady hand to a turning wheel
Grinding the grinders away.
I ask, and am born,
Now, and to come.

What day is this on which we are gathered to listen?

It is a day of quarrels and a day of sin.
The rain rushes into the already overflowing gutters.
The preachers are shouting in tongues we cannot interpret.
The automobiles strike at many angles to let death in.
The revolutionists scream at each other in hatreds not to cease.
It is an ordinary day in an American city.
In His Wounds is our peace.

The Curtains

Under the rooftops
The curtains gather,
Relics of looking
For a sign of beauty
To surmount the gathered
Ugly sleepings
In hot weathers,
Flesh slick with water,
The upper bedrooms
Heavy with dreams
Of broken fences.

The Dreamers

The idle lovers
Dream of leather
Or cologne bottles
In autumn storerooms.
The magazines tell them,
"Dream me. Dream me."
The eternal waters
Darken inward.

The Collectors

The money has been paid.
The turnstile of the wide town turns,
Remnants of snow, black-flaked, on the stairway.
The turnstile turns and permits to enter
The man in blue jeans and an army jacket,
The man with thinning hair and several school books,
The delicate man in the pale blue jacket,
The Puerto Rican with his lunchbox and the harassed Canadian,
Graven images in their untoward hearts.

In the wet streets the waiting taxis are ready.
From the taxis the drivers call out to each other
In languages they can scream but do not understand.

The women in the apartment houses are making themselves ready,
Eyes darkened, cheeks reddened in a fever of hurry,
Having forgotten the hours when they are expected to embark.

The man-damaged snow descends on the city's dark.

The Tribunal Must, in Due Course, Come to Order

If a clock falters, why should that interrupt your betrayals?
If a skull bleaches in the desert sun, what does that have to do
      with the town?
The revolutions are applauded in the mirrors.
The mirrors revolve, and turn down.

For the New Year

Seeds sing.
Snow holds
Only in patches.
The rains have fled.
Blue winter shines.
I resolve
In blue silence
To discern
A flame of blue silence
To sing.

I have written much of death
In varied ways
For reasons better known to an invited spirit
Than to me.
To say, "Death is nearer"
Is a building stone.
In our father's house
There are many workrooms.
This is known.
I resolve
In blue silence
To sing.

Rest easy. Your slumber is to be undisturbed
except perhaps
by
a voice quietly accepting your presence with a soft answer (o
        turn away, wrath!)
or by
the drift of a waterfall which is a sound more than a misting
or by
an Indian walker walking in the snow with an almost undetectable
        lightness
or by
the rustling of a circular which announces your name and an
        unstated reward.
Who pays it? by what currency of what country?
The snowbanks shift in the mountains according to natural law.

A Garden Is an Enclosure for a While

The garden needs a door.

How else let out the rabbits
   and the turtle
   and the hawk
      with the damaged wing?

How else let in the sunlight
   if the garden
   proceeds to darken?

How else wave your hand
   at the passengers
   in the stage coach?

(To greet them from the wall
   would be considered
      eccentric.)

How else beg
   at the door?

A Breastplate

I took a wish into a famished railroad.
I separated a wish with a wind-sharp carving knife.
I wished for a boat and a hammock and a wish-board.
The tawdry and the usual I wished twice.

Then came a different wish.
I opened my mouth to the soap
In a tray, to a weed in a gutter sneaked over,
To a cloud delivering a rain-calling
As the gravel blistered my spent heel
In the driveway, in the moorings, in the hurry of the dead.

Too many have died for me to be telling.
Each gravity of failure adds its stroke,
Those who meet it, those who fumble into it, those who will it
            persistently.
Failure is to be not in, not to be in, not to declare
The knock of the stranger or his echo on the stair,
Or to loiter there.

What is to be done is done.
What is to be done is to do.
What is for love is now.
What is to be known is true.

I promise you.

The Hours

For Roland D. Carter

The book of hours
Has a cipher
To be broken.

The illuminations
In the margins
Touch its music.

Rains wash
Not far
Away.

The book of hours
Turns its pages
On our coaxing.

A dancer enters.
He will bow
And dance away.

An hour readies
In the silence
We have misspoken.

A hand has touched
The pages
Of the day.

The Angels

The angels take approaches. Some enter by root
And others cloud-following, cloud-brightening, come.
Some in street clothes walk a gloomy one or two miles
And do not enter conversations, but watch trees,
City soot, gables that are cracked with many snows,
And limp into a bar, and hear each word which speaks
Even with broken love to cheer them as they turn,
And look into the empty mirrors, and depart.
And there are lovely angels which touch young faces;
These are as necessary to us as breathing
And words rarely capture the approach of their wings.
And there are great angels on great hills when wars come
Who know so much about justice they grow weary
But hold their beautiful adamant swords steady
And have such endurance we have great need of them.
And there are others who can do nothing but stand
In a given place and enter water and trees,
Wooden benches, a turn of weed-fixed light, a stone
White barred with grey and singular in its standing.
At certain hours one can view their plain, their sacred
Countenances. These are the ones whom I know best,
My companions, my intercessors, and my friends.

The Canyon

The seraph, flame by flame, descended.
The rocks foundered.
The gate cracked
And the red stone.
This is the desert!
This is the messenger,
   messenger,
   messenger.
Stone.

Fog Days for Great Cranberry Island

I

Many maps have retained the coast
Of the coast as maps retain.
Daily the radio has reported fog,
Vinalhaven, Ellsworth, Sutton's Island.
Maine.

The sun is the ghost, the unreal
Claimant, the straddler, the hurrier,
The eye,
Struggler, avoider, retainer,
The passer-by.

Sun is the reality beyond the fog.
This is established by precedents, by beholders,
By the clear view memory needs.

In the cold shallows, swim.
To avoid: sea urchins, barnacles, glass.
In sunshine the water is cold.
In fog, it blurs, the arm, wet, rising, swims in a softer wet,
Continuous, less cold.

The wounds of time are near.

II

Be restive where you are.
The withering spends
Its indistinct sad echo
As you know.

The care you heave is you.
The shoulder pinches, lungs

Strain, and the boats depart
Along the cuts and rock-ways of the coast.
Shall we discern the grave?

Reported: even graves are caught by fog.
It seeps gradually far enough.
The markers float in a field
Barely visible, barely
Accessible.
Or not.

The sun days, brief and overdue,
Drift in the woods they fade into.
And on the south end of the island still mist, then fog.
There has been mist on the place of the Prussian lady,
Born Dorethea Albertina
Called Hannah Caroline.

When she heard her husband had died in the Arctic, she threw his
          stuffed seals into the bay.
Whether out of grief or hatred, it is too late to say.

Five Emblems for Lent

The crabbed dark
Speaks its thorn.

The ghosted sumac
Tenders in foglight
Other branches
Than are seen.

The shadowing pines yield
(As the flame
Of blue clear bell notes
In a snow-lit field)
What sleep permits,
What love.

The retreat of a distant
Pale enormous cloud sweetness
Which was near.

We planted, but did not foretell
The resisting grief
Broken, in hiding, in the planted rows
And the risen leaf.

In a Train Station at 3 a.m. a Man Sits Quietly and Afraid

Smoke countering rain.
A hunger for persimmons.
The slight taste of blood
On the back of your fist.
Tones of a cold bell.
A face in a newspaper.
The sough of a sandal's
Arrest.

The Clock Hands

I

The bicycle shop closing down.
Glass in a field broken to sun.
Woods piling leaves of unseen many colors.
The frail tissue of repose.
The stroke of the clock hand on the pinched nerve.
Alcohol, nurses, cold.
In the dream no purchase was awarded,
No signpost
Scanned.

II

"Did you mail the photograph?"
                                    "No, sir.
It was too late to bargain."
"A cousin was it?"
                                    "Distant."
"In a distant city?"
"Or some other shallow."

III

A cipher derides you.
An unpaid bill hammers.
A late snow dampens
The scar on the thumbprint,
Blurring the remnant.
A hid door closes,
One, then another.

The Judges

They deposit the black cloaks in the square.
The rummage is not for sale.
March, and a trickle of wind
And a woman is washing in the air the black cloaks.
Her hands are blunt, her fingers rapidly working.
The expression is almost delicate
On her aging and strong features.
Pleasure lingers there as she washes
Only in air the garments
So that in the morning the judges
May sit in the black cloaks judging
The quality of her work.
Their decision will be final
As always.

The torch is carried homeward by the runner.
It is a fine day in the town square
And the girls, in how many colors!,
Await the end of his journey.
If he were less exhausted, the victory
Would have more meaning to him.
The judges sit inside the windows
Unapplauding
As always.

The girl stands at the fork of the lightly travelled roads.
There are other towns to walk to, but she does not know their
        names.
On one road a young man is waiting

In clean work clothes and with freshly scrubbed fingernails,
Six four and unbelievably handsome.
He is certain to adore and protect her.
On the other road the judges are gathered
In their black garments
To give her their instructions
As always.

If on a summer night they would remember
A summer night, if on a feast day
They would carry baskets to the farmers,
If they had one green ribbon to give to a girl's young lover,
If they would give one jump and a kick sideways at the approach
            of a victorious runner,
Then they would fold their black garments carefully
And they would dance—I do not exaggerate it—they would
            dance in the town's square wildly
Raising the dust with the whoop of their kicking and yelling
Making the housewives close windows before the advent of the
            dust clouds
(Meanwhile the children would scurry towards the jelly
            cupboards).
But they do not remember a summer night
And they do not carry baskets,
And if they overhear any marked or ironic comment
On their standing in the community
Or the nature of their sober habits,
Their judgment will be as final
As always.

The Heart Dark-All-Round

For Esther V. Hansen

The heart, mighty of darkness, cloudy in its breast
(Who sees within the rib cage? What light is there?)
Clamors, is great and is great speaking, fond of dark
Sayings that fit the cavity in which it dwells.

Do not yield it to mind completely. It knows how
To claim its own, whose pace is heavy of blood.
When you ignore it, or evade it, is it tamed?
It has no great hurry. It glistens in its silence.

Are we of it or it of us? Neither and both.
Is it mankind, brute kind, or something that is other?
It is the heart. It is as old as Homer who
Sang matchlessly of it. Blind, it endures all things.

The Edge of the City

In a place of dreams slow fires are scattered.
Avoiding the smoldering, men strive for
A ribless umbrella, a chipped windshield,
A girl's no longer perfumed handkerchief,
A diary's illegible wet pages
(Look at them fall! too sodden to flutter),
A fishhook twisted past any fishing,
An abandoned national flag (name it),
A blackened and wickless kerosene lamp,
For the stain only on a tablecloth,
For things dead, for things rotten, for the waste
Of the fighting. Stubbornly, they enter
The smoke, then the fires, and do not notice.
They do not conceive their pain, nor may we.
They have no hunger, only their firm choice
To quarrel, crying out, "Mine! Mine! Justice!"

To Neighbors, Who Will Not Receive a Copy

The neighbors, who have been accused of murder,
   are standing in the sunlight
      their hands vacant of weapons.

Hello! you who are standing in the sunlight,
   did you murder others
      who were standing in the sunlight?

You do peddle drugs
   which feed
   abundant death.

Why do you cluster
   like friends
      with your cameras?

Why does sunlight shine
   like innocence
      on the heads and hands of betrayers?

I have not lifted my hands
   in greeting
      or in recognition.

I do not plan to proclaim
   a complicity
      in your guilt.

The Flowers

The flowers, in newspaper bundles,
In large red slightly rusty tins
Are present for selling.

The blind woman who sells them
Looks peaceful
In the slant of Washington sunlight.

The parking lots are dangerous
In the evening.
Bodies are torn against their will;
Mouths are prevented from screaming.

In the Senate Office Building
A few blocks away
Armed robbers have succeeded in plain daylight.

The decisions affect
The bankers and the steam rollers
And the Pakistan tortures.

Why should not the
Beautiful automobiles
Drive slowly up the
Embassy drives?

It is good to arrive safely
After dark,
Even if the apartment is lonely,
Especially when it rains.

The Planting

We came of country people. Plow us true.
A nation learns too slowly how to ask.
We fear the dying that we have to do.
Lord, set our hearts upon our proper task.

Suppose a Country Gave a Holiday and
Then Suppose That the Tears Were True

The rhododendron blossoms. The water continuously falls.

The crowds are not coming close, only to the plaque by the rail.

The swimmers are advancing arm by arm in the pool formed by
the rocks at the foot of the waterfall.

If your presence were not required, I would not be holding your
hand.

The musicians are beginning to tune their instruments. There are
flags by the bandstand.

The Island

Cranberries by the moss.
The ferns touching air.
Mussels on the rocks
Where the waves were.
Lichen and flounder and deer.

And sleep like the breaking of bread.

The lovers are sleeping and the clowns are sleeping and the water glistens on the rocks and the clowns are waking and the lovers are stirring and the water glistens on the rocks and it is morning and the lovers are waking and the streets become crowded and the clowns are striding and beginning to whistle and the water glistens on the rocks.

In a Cedar Wind

It is a time to quieten, as
Lovers witness by a pond.
A rain-bent bulrush lifts its head.
The broken cedar boughs show forth
The recent storm which has blown away.
Lighten! and the winds obey.
Stillness narrows toward a birth.
Cloud white! cloud white! the birds begin.
Further on is into day.

The Reeds

The reeds spoke in the early dark
Of a music of returning
And a pace to travel to.
Is your return by flashlight? Are you known?
What trespass did you do?
Stone happens in the valley to be broken.
The stars reach the valley before you.

Crowds

The crowds are expecting the event at the airport.
They have gathered and have covered the runways and the
                 observation decks.
The balloonist therefore despairs of making the landing.
He descends in a plowed field in a cheerful solitude.

Apart from the streetways, apart from the strident
Unmeasured incessant bickering of women,
He purchases the venison with his last silver dollar.
He lights the fire carefully in the presence of wind.

A Letter in Mid-February

The cold wave descends, cold.
The winter rain freezes on the trees
  though only yesterday
  the sun was brilliant
  and the air warm.
I have thought of apples
  in an orchard hidden from the railroad.
I would have despaired some time back
  had I not remembered the clear
  thrumming of water.
We must carry a winter supply of coal
  to the house, one room with boarded windows
  by the winter railroad
  where for several years
  the thrumming of the approaching trains
  has not been heard.
I would have carried water
  sooner
  had you told me.
I am asking that you remember this letter
  when we touch hands
  crossing the railroad
  to the remembered path
  up the winter hill.
The quiet rocks shine
  with ice
  on the hill.

The Progress

This is my dream. I am walking toward a rusted, barbed, unspoken gate.

I open the gate.

The gate complains in a bored dim voice of the intruders whose names have been scrubbed off the hinges.

Accomplished, rough, handsome, virtually unaging, I ask for my credit cards and am refused.

I explain carefully why the letters recommending me are mocking.

The reply is a silence which I decide to applaud.

In the white chalk dust the ruler is ready for measuring any query I may write on the blackboard in the precise middle of the harassed afternoon.

Under the windows of the classroom the gates are being carried off, strapped down with metal, on the flat cars.

The train turns into a siding
toward the gate.

The Clockwork

The clockwork was presented to the Mayor with the bomb key shorn, the fingerprints identified, the arrests made, and the detectives ticketed for promotion.

The Mayor put the clockwork on the conference table, explaining its function and the competence displayed in cutting the wires in the precisely necessary order at the decidedly necessary time.

There was gentle applause. The council sat plumply about the table.

The clock ticked in the hall.

The Explanation

"This opaque projection is a diagram of the train wreck.
The mistakes are calculable and should not recur.
The switchman was no more responsible than the computer.
In the diagram the switchman is designated iota and the computer
is designated pi—
You! old sir on the second row, why are you interrupting?"

"There were other winds than those recorded at the siding.
They said, 'Die.' "

Realities for an Advent Season

My sons quarrel about the car. It is almost as warm as summer.
Sleep enters now. The Russians are ahead.
The cities breathe slag of our hungers.
Our hungers need rest and the tendrils grow backward
Along a slow creek with stones for wet crossing
Or further on, a bridge which sways on cables.
My father and I quarrel about the car. It is summer.
How can it have been summer when there is still quarreling?
What energy holds the water under the surface?
The surface bobs like a drowning head.
Sleep enters. Sleep enters. It was summer.
I drove the car along the crest road in the summer.
She slept on my shoulder for a while.
It is only for a while that your woman sleeps on your shoulder.
It will only be for a while that the Russians are ahead.
I am quarreling about the car with my father.
My father is dead.

An Evening Colloquy

"Tear out the things,
Root and branch,
That are not of your peace."

"I am in my way,
Root and branch,
And can reach no peace."

"Behind your shadow,
Tangle of dark and air,
Light is of your peace."

"I cannot see to approach.
The roots are bedded deep.
The branches stand in night air.
I desire my peace."

"Then let the tree be watered by
Such hunger and thirst
That the tree die,
Be rooted into peace."

"I am afraid to die."

"So was I,
Who am the Crown of Peace."

Ascension

A Dream

I gladdened. It was noon.
Cicadas' lily song
Was delicate to hear
And dry and sweet the tone.
I rested by a spring.
Sleep faded into stone
And all seemed all was well
Within the resting ear.
I woke. I was alone.

I stood in a bare yard.
A ghostly poverty
Descended, out of place,
Where cast and cold things lay,
Where interference thrived,
Reviling, evil-tongued,
Its claimants and their pain.
I cried against the cold.
A shadow struck, and stayed.

I saw the moon retreat.
My name was in my way.
The branches blackly stung.
The way was into fear.
Discordantly I swam
A river green with sedge
Until the dream was paid

In figures of its coin.
And then cold dawn swam near.

So shadows came apart.
Is vacancy a tune?
Another said me "no."
The day ascends the sky,
And sky is white with heat.
The waters shall repeat
The avenues they climbed.
Does blood fall back? It falls.
A sparrow sings me home.

Images for the Gospel of Christ

If one revolves a vine-enamored thumb
Against the grape, a smoothness comes of it.
The wine is after, decorously dark,
And after after, madnesses, the stark
Ingraining seizures that have left men dumb
Or speaking tongues which have a share of wit
Akin to rage, or rage's counterfeit.

Or it is like a sea. No plank to shore
Men up, no compass there, a place to swim
Where strong waves range and indolently flash.
Or like a coal of fire. Or like a gash
Still living, winking out inclement gore
That vanishes where mossy earth grows dim
And slow roots alter what they take of Him.

Or like the quiet music of our need,
Or like a thawing brook whose waters run
Silver and slow. Or like a pearl of price
That pays for all we are and shall suffice
At the far edge of death. Or like a seed
That grows as silently as it is sown.
Or like a walk on Sunday in the sun.

A Summary in Three Parts

The invitation arrived by unexpected mail.
The quality of the paper is not a certain indication of the
    rank of the host, but suggests that he is a citizen of
    no ordinary city.
To reply promptly would be considered a courtesy.
Any delay could be costly and in truth could prove fatal.

The sowers are broadcasting their seed on thorn, rock, and soil.
In the nearby barn the harvesters are preparing their sickles.
The pearl locked in a drawer is only potentially valuable.
The darnel is well rooted and confident to flourish.
The whores are as desirable as ever, but the young man has run
    out of money.
The lost coin glimmers by the wayside.

The Master is coming.

Treasure

We came at night, by river, to the foot
Of cliffs that worked the river's foam to mud.
The sand was ruined; grey water was the root
Of marsh grass pale as grey stone scoured of blood.

We tied the boat and climbed steep ways. We found
The coarse vines snarled across a ledge of clay.
The river's plunging body deepened sound.
Our eyes that gave on darkness turned away.

The mark the map relinquished told the cave,
A dagger planted in an X of wood.
We gazed upon it, and our bodies gave
A legend credence in the tideward blood.

The pirate brought here with a fiercer lust
Than wine or body takes, his share of gold,
And made the darkness steward of his trust,
Companionate with silence and with cold.

We shook our fear as one might shake a child,
Pulled back the vines and entered, crazed with love
Of gold we sought in darkness, reconciled
To ways that fit the darkness like a glove.

The map was accurate. We paced. We found
The rotten wood, the wine remains, the rest.

The bones in shallow order held their ground.
The snake's skull rested on the empty breast.

For love or fear of God we shoveled deep
In fury masked as warning for his pride
And offered to the passive clay to keep
What once had kept a world at bay, but died.

We stuttered out a prayer above his bones,
Then climbed in earth, in dim light felt our way,
And heaved the chest beyond the foaming stones
And heard the waters on the high cliffs play.

A Bank of Laurel

I came for weeds.
I came for the thorns,
    the thick web of hurt branches,
    not laurel and not the water.
I came to be seen. There is no one to tell it to.
Not a rock but was there.

Or put it differently. I do not want your explanation
    of my hurt.

Or like this. I went, let me remember,
    for laurel and for water and for moss,
    for delicacy of beauty and its variations.

Only
    having arrived,
        I touched the laurel and
        she entangled me
        and her white fingers were hurrying
        among my fingers and my hair and
        her thighs went across me suddenly
        at the edge of the water,
        and I was grateful and we lay content with each other

only
    I could not share her cold refusal to weep,
        which has persisted.

That is an old story, you tell me,
    and you say I do not have it straight.

47

I have told to you what it was that happened.
    I wept tears, a crowd of them,
        and they grew, I am sure of it,
        the thorn I am fond of.

I am still looking for those thorns
    in the dry wood.

Only
    as I search for them, I come across laurel.

The Deserted Walker in the Deserted Streets of a Far Town

The gloom is despotic, the air cold.
In a crowd of fragrance, who was to tell the time?
In a black and white dress in an afternoon coffee shop
You drank coffee with me; it was later the freezing rains began.
The rain is beginning to freeze now and I continue to walk, with
    caution.
The streets are becoming more dangerous every falling minute:
The cars will slide into guy wires and into store fronts
And when the windows are broken the mannequins will be
    exposed
To the drifting of the freezing rain on their black and white
    dresses.
The rain beats on my eyes, but I can still discover
The street to the coffee shop where my hunger began
And I could if I wished follow the highway to the motel.
On the highway there will be cars sliding into the embankments,
And the freezing rain will continue against the windows of the
    motel
Until at one open window a face will begin to scream
Soundlessly at the distance from which I will be listening,
Calling no doubt one of the names I was never allowed to learn.
And on the lakefront the snow will be excessive
After the freezing rains and the withdrawals of the pleasure boats
And no water skiers will be seen on the water and no fires upon
    the hillsides
And I shall think of you with me once in a small cottage in the
    mountains.
As for your infidelities, they have been absconded.

After all I was one of your infidelities so by what right do I
         complain?
As for your suicide, the psychiatrist has already explained that.
I continue to look for you; the centuries freeze in the rain.

The Broken Lumber

In the yard near the barn is the pile of lumber,
A heap of boards, rot at them, nails clenched, the nails with rust,
Disorder in the splintered long boundaries of the crossed masses.
A careless mind let them pile so.
What deserted them is not spoken in them.
In sleep sometimes I see them. Sleep is a forbearance.
You and I, hand in hand, have walked near them. We have walked
To a barbed-wire, tumbledown, nettle-clambered fence.
We have looked toward the lumber, grieved at such boundaries.
The boards which we saw then flowed toward one color
Except for a few spots, the knots, the big nails, the rust in them.
The second summer we came here we were told the story,
Told it by several people who live year round in the valley,
That there were two here, man and wife, at love and quarreling,
Hand in hand, walking in the wide yard, turning them houseward.
            We imagine it:
The long rains, the mud roads. Even hot dust would have seemed
            companionable,
But there was mud of clay, mud heavy on spokes, mud on
            weathered boots.
Late winter, and the saw screeching into a warped board of the
            mud road leading
Elsewhere! Screaming it!
And he threw the saw down, heard the way screaming, and took
            it.
The next night a neighbor saw at a long distance the light move,

The hay of the barn burning! The rain stopped it. The barn was
      not badly damaged.
They did not find a sign of departure except the broken lantern.

We hear more from the inhabitants. I offer an explanation.
Suppose in the woods near the farm a muskrat eye is staring
By the ice of a stream, the water moving, sluggish,
A sluggish muskrat eye staring at the snow of the forest.
Suppose that such an eye, disused to limitation,
Stares where the past blurs into the ice and the water,
And suppose in a late sycamore crying and anguished
The nameless foregatherers of the stream's cold arrival
Crying the hurt of winter. The neighbors tell the story
Of the saw (it approaches pure rust in the woodshed)
Night upon night sounding, screeching in inadequate venturing
Into the board heap, leaving no mark except for the grain of its
      noise,
Long in the long nights for the countryside's wide listening
Screeching, sawing, and faint under the saw noise the sound of
      voices quarreling,
And faintly, clearly seen, the flames lighting along the empty and
      weathering barn,
The black shadow of the light upon the broken lumber.

A Story about Ghosts

We were supposed to keep the ghosts
  in that house on the mountain
    but we somehow let them escape

Perhaps on a wet afternoon
  when we were sleeping
    in a retreated dream

Perhaps at a party
  when the restless glitter
    of feminine voices
  began to sprinkle
    over the ash trays

Perhaps into snow
  or into steam

Or it may even be that
  the ghosts, being lonely ghosts,
    had clung to deprivation,
  to the angry, sour, mosslike film
      in the walls and in the attic
  but when you brought kindness
      the house changed
  and the ghosts were of course free to leave.

Perhaps we shall meet them yet
  in a snow-capped inn
    in a good weather.

Perhaps they shall smile
  and be seen.

A Realm

Teach us these stones.
Our hands bleed for possession.
The hills and orange flowers
Overlook our approaches.
Softer than the perfect seed
Of expectation,
The lichens await us
In the Atlantic morning.

Fish into streams.
In their cool wanderings
Snows remain
From the heights of passage.
Change enters change gently,
As once the tears you let me see
Resist departure, blessedly.

Linger the waste of the snow.
Enter the eye's preparing.
A small realm shines
Till at its limit, a seed
Glimmers, appearing.

Ask if its weather be soon.

The Music

An unsleeping music
        keeps on coming.

The nervous shadows
        do not stay.

Alive! alive!
        is at the rescue.

A morning wagon
        rides away.

From a Theological Primer

Your hand is numbered.

Every bone?

The tiniest bone and ganglion,
The minute feathering of a bird,
Pine needles' shadows, and of each cloud
The instantaneous waverings.

And every word?

Is known.

A Convalescence

The time wavered. Pain made a stiff entry.
I woke the next day, deliriums gone.
Outside were voices unutterable.
I made joy, I was gladness, I heard them,
Every place speaking out its singleness,
Its proximity's surface of motion,
Gladly as a clear bell windily strikes,
As a child's kite successfully rises,
Odd as the spider climbing the doorsill,
Treasured as any treasure imagined
Or hoped for. A peacefulness unclouded
The white bedclothes, the mirror, the windows,
The fish pond, the back door, and every place.

To Be Posted by a Kitchen Window

Lord, bless the shadows on the wall.
Bless the afternooning sun.
Bless the gates and the gravestones.
Bless the crows on the lawn.
Bless the apples when they fall.
Bless our sleep before it comes.

Dream us rains.

Antiphon

Who commands here?

No one, sir. We're singing.

Who leads the song?

No one, sir. We're praising.

What praising then?

The least of voice.
We hear him cry
As a cricket might
In a distant tree
On a cold starred night,
Cry gently as a stream in turning
Around a small rock
In the wavered light
Daylong, nightlong
In a December night.

This very night?

This very night.

Paul Ramsey, born in Atlanta, has taught and lived in Alabama, New York, Minnesota, and California. He is currently Poet-in-Residence and Alumni Distinguished Service Professor at the University of Tennessee at Chattanooga. Mr. Ramsey is well-known as poet, critic, scholar, and teacher. He has been widely published in this country as well as Canada, England, Italy, Wales, and India. He has won a number of awards including the SAMLA Studies Award in 1968 for his book *The Art of John Dryden.* Among his other books of poetry are *Triptych, In an Ordinary Place, A Window for New York,* and *The Doors.*